BY WHING
TO
PORT SODERICK

DOUGLAS HEAD ELECTRIC TRAMWAY, ISLE OF MAN.

THE STORY OF THE MANX MARINE DRIVE

GEORGE HOBBS

Loaghtan Books
Caardee
Dreemskerry Hill
Maughold
Isle of Man
IM7 1BE

Published by Loaghtan Books

First published: May 2015

Copyright © George Hobbs, 2015

Typesetting and origination by:
Loaghtan Books

Printed and bound by:
Lavenham Press

Website: www.loaghtanbooks.com

ISBN: 978 1 908060 12 9

Photographic copyright © George Hobbs, 2015
unless otherwise stated

For Geoff Gartside
Thanks for the encouragement!

Front cover: Past and present at the site of the Douglas Head tram terminus

Rear cover: The grand archway which still stands marking the start of the Marine Drive

Title page: Edwardian postcard of a Douglas Southern tram crossing a sea cove on the Walberry viaduct

Contents page: Illustrations from a set of stamps issued by the Isle of Man post office in 1988

Page 4: Extracts from late nineteenth- and early twentieth-century guide books

CONTENTS

Douglas

DOUGLAS HEAD MARINE DRIVE
and
ELECTRIC TRAMWAYS

uation of this Tramway is, in some respects, unique. It com-
ces at Douglas Head, 150 feet above the sea. It then follows
as Head Marine Drive (the cutting of which has opened out
most beautiful views of the precipitous and broken
m Douglas coast-line of the Island), in a southerly direction,
t Soderick, undulating, but continually rising until Walberry
versa. is reached, about 300 feet above the sea. The
Scenery along this portion is excessively wild and
rocks rising precipitously 150 feet above the track on the
d falling almost straight into the sea on the other. Con-
Tramway crosses

s run every
minutes.

ristal and
k.

ce and very
uch as find natural beauty
drive or walk than
the routes enumerated above are interesting,
Beautiful Marine Drive (a) should on no account be
missed. A good round of about 6 miles is by the Drive,
returning by the footpath to the Castletown road (c).

(a) BY MARINE DRIVE

The stretch of rocky coast south of Douglas Head is equal
to anything that Cornwall can show. The cliffs rise in places
more than 300 feet, and are broken by deep, rugged gorges,
across which viaducts have been thrown to carry the Drive.
In hardly any other place in Great Britain is rock scenery
of such grandeur so accessible. Even the celebrated drive
round Great Orme's Head at Llandudno is surpassed by this.
From the viaducts one looks down on jagged projections
and the most extraordinary contortions of strata, while far

A SEA PEEP AT PORT SODERICK

INTRODUCTION

In its heyday as a holiday destination, one of the Isle of Man's most pleasurable excursions was a trip from Douglas to the thriving resort of Port Soderick about four miles to the south. The resort could be reached by train, by coastal steamer or by a journey along the Marine Drive.

At the end of the nineteenth century a number of resorts developed marine drives. One of the better known examples is that around the Great Orme in Llandudno, North Wales. The Welsh Marine Drive is about the same length as the Manx one but differs in being circular. It opened in 1878 as a carriage road, with tolls payable to the private owner. The Llandudno Marine Drive is still a toll road but it is now under the control of the local council. Spectacular views over the cliffs unfold during the circuit of the Great Orme.

Scarborough, North Yorkshire, also has a Marine Drive, rather shorter at 1300 yards, and remaining close to sea level as it follows the coast in north-east England below the castle. Storm damage during construction delayed the opening of this drive until 1908, construction having started in 1897.

Neither the Llandudno nor the Scarborough Marine Drives were graced by tramways, although trams terminated at the start of Scarborough's drive. The Great Orme Cable Tramway, which opened on 31 July 1902, continues to provide a seasonal service to the top of the Great Orme but makes no use of the marine drive. On a clear day the Great Orme

An old postcard view of a busy day at Douglas Head. Coming round the curve is a motor plus trailer car set of the Douglas Southern Electric Tramway, just starting its journey to Port Soderick

Another postcard view of Douglas Harbour with one of the Incline Railway Cars at the lower terminus and one of the harbour ferries at work bringing pleasure seekers across the harbour

can be seen from the Isle of Man. Previously a steamer service ran between Llandudno and Douglas, but this has not operated for many years.

The Douglas Head Marine Drive was cut into the cliffs and visitors could take a carriage ride, enjoy a pleasant walk whilst admiring the views, or make the journey onboard an electric tram. Cliff lifts at both ends of the Drive facilitated access to and from Douglas and Port Soderick. A thriving business existed as there was always the option of returning to town by one of the alternative means of transport, and indeed many pleasure seekers chose to do that.

Port Soderick offered a wide selection of attractions including cafés, bars, beach, smugglers' cave, camera obscura, ice cream kiosks and other enterprises designed to entertain tourists and relieve them of their cash.

Sadly, all this is in the past. The Isle of Man Railway still operates a summer train service and Port Soderick station lies on the Douglas to Port Erin line. The *MV Karina* puts in occasional appearances in Port Soderick harbour. The tramway, the cliff lifts and all the other Port Soderick attractions have closed. Although a bus service operated along the Marine Drive for some years, this was also discontinued as cliff instabilities led to the closure of the road to all but foot and bicycle traffic almost forty years ago. The once bustling resort and the coast road from Douglas are now quiet. However, the sea air along the Marine Drive is just as invigorating and the views may now be enjoyed in peace as part of the *Raad ny Foillan* (Way of the Seagull) coastal footpath.

This book tells the story of the Marine Drive and its tramway. Hopefully it will encourage the reader to explore and view the relics of a past era. It is an easy walk of around four miles from Douglas and best enjoyed in the morning when the sun shines on the east of the island.

To reach the start of the Marine Drive at Douglas Head from Douglas town centre, today's traveller has several options. By road, Head Road (or more strictly Fort Anne Road) can be reached either by crossing the harbour entrance by the modern lifting bridge and turning right along South Quay, or by crossing the Stone Bridge at the head of the harbour and turning back along South Quay. Head Road climbs steeply past Fort Anne to Douglas Head. By foot walkers have a couple more options. After walking along the South Quay to the Battery Pier they may take a path running parallel to the course of the former Douglas Head Incline Railway and past the now restored Great Union Camera Obscura, which is one of the few attractions on Douglas Head that is now open. Alternatively a stepped footpath leading from the South Quay joins Head Road near Fort Anne.

The options were rather more varied when tourist traffic was far heavier.

Douglas Head ferry

Douglas Head Steam Ferries Ltd. was founded on 23 March 1897 and the new company immediately ordered three double-ended, four-propeller steam ferries from Dee Shipbuilding and Engineering of Queensferry in Flint, North Wales. The vessels were 59ft long (measured at the waterline, 66ft overall) with a beam of 18ft and draught of 6ft and were 48.8 gross tons. Each vessel was licensed to carry 350 passengers. Two of the vessels, *Rose* and *Shamrock*, entered service later that year but the third, *Thistle*, did not arrive until 1898. The names derived from the national flowers of England, Ireland and Scotland. No *Daffodil* for Wales, despite the ships having been built in that country.

The steam ferries provided a service between the Victoria Pier on the north side of Douglas Harbour and the Battery Pier on the south side, a distance of about a quarter of a mile. This saved a walk of around three-quarters of a mile, assuming that the swing bridge, which was on the site of the current lifting bridge, was open for pedestrian traffic, or of more than a mile by the Stone Bridge and the inner harbour. A toll was charged at the swing bridge, so why not enjoy a pleasant boat trip? The ferries operated seasonally between Easter and September and proved very popular, carrying over 500,000 passengers per year. Turnstiles located on the Battery Pier collected the single fare of 1d and no fares were collected on the boats. Later, through-tickets to Port Soderick by ferry, The Douglas Head Incline Railway, The Douglas Southern Electric Tramway and The Port Soderick Incline Railway could be purchased from a kiosk on the Victoria Pier.

During the First World War the ferry service was suspended. Although there are as yet no known records of the boats' usage during the war, *Thistle* was lost whilst in Admiralty service off Aberdeen on 23 November 1916. Presumably the Admiralty had requisitioned *Thistle*, and possibly the other ferry boats, for war service. Their excellent manoeuvrability would have made them useful in restricted waterways.

After the war the harbour ferry recommenced service for the 1919 season at an increased single fare of 2d. After several years delay by the directors, a replacement *Thistle* was delivered from W. J. Yarwood of Northwich, Cheshire, England in 1926. Although shorter, the new *Thistle* was larger than the original boats at 54ft long (measured at the waterline, 65ft overall), 22.6ft wide and 6.9ft draught and 67 tons gross. Her licensed passenger capacity was 430, although this was later reduced to 400. The service was then generally provided by *Rose* and *Thistle*, *Shamrock* being used as a floating landing stage at the Battery Pier.

During the 1930s the ferries continued to be profitable. However, in common with the Marine Drive Tramway, the decline in tourism reduced both income and profitability and led to reduced shareholder dividends. Services were again

This Edwardian postcard shows a busy day at the Victoria Pier, Douglas. Three steamships are clearly visible as are a line of carriages waiting for hire. Moored to the right of the Victoria Pier are two of the Douglas Head steam ferries; the advertisements on the ends for toffee are very prominent and apparently more important than the vessels' names, or indeed the brand of toffee being promoted (Mackintoshes). The landing stage at the Battery Pier below Douglas Head is off the right of the picture

suspended during the Second World War and *Rose* and *Thistle* were chartered out. Based in Londonderry, they were used to disembark servicemen from US troopships. *Shamrock* was sold for scrap in 1940, being broken up in Douglas during 1942. After the war the harbour ferry did not immediately resume operation. *Rose* and *Thistle* returned after war service, but were laid up in Castletown Harbour before being transferred to a new company, Douglas Head Ferry Ltd., on 28 May 1949. Unfortunately *Rose's* boiler failed to gain a new certificate, but *Thistle* re-entered service in June 1949.

Meanwhile Douglas Corporation had started a bus service to the Battery Pier from the bus station, which provided direct competition for the ferry trade. The increasing cost of coal, bus competition and decreasing tourist trade meant that the steamboat service was uneconomic, especially with a vessel large enough to carry 400 passengers. *Thistle* was sold at the end of the 1950 season; sadly she foundered under tow *en route* to her new owners, Pembrokeshire County Council in south Wales, and sank. Douglas Head Ferry continued with three smaller wooden motor boats. The continued decline in tourism in the following years led to decreasing services and there has been no harbour ferry service since the early 1970s. Meanwhile *Rose* was laid up in Douglas Harbour until she was broken up around 1970. Although inactive for twenty-five years, *Rose* had outlasted her sisters and nearly lasted for the duration of the ferry service itself.

The Douglas Head Incline Railway

A short climb uphill from the Battery Pier was the Douglas Head Incline Railway's lower station. The cliff lift ran up past the Great Union Camera Obscura to the top of Douglas Head itself. The lift was arranged in the usual fashion where two separate tracks each carried one car with a connecting cable which allowed the weight of the descending car to assist the upward journey of its fellow.

The Incline Railway opened in August 1900 and thereafter ran during the summer seasons. The line was 450ft long with an average inclination of 1 in 4.5. Unusually for a cliff lift the line was not straight, there being a slight bend about one third of the way up. An oil-powered engine at the upper terminus drove the cable which was attached to the cars. Hurst Nelson of Motherwell, Scotland, who were well-known manufacturers of tramcars and railway wagons, supplied the two cars.

With the outbreak of the First World War in August 1914 the tourist traffic ceased abruptly and the Incline Railway

Right: the lower station of the Douglas Cliff Incline Railway around 1954, some time after closure but before removal of the rails and cars for scrap. The two cars are parked half-way up the line, just above the curve. (Courtesy of Travel Lens Photographic) Below: the course of the Incline Railway is still evident sixty years later. 11 October 2014

Above: looking down the Incline Railway from below the Great Union Camera Obscura the two disused cars are again seen parked on the line. (Courtesy of Travel Lens Photographic)
Right: a more recent view shows the location of the cliff lift relative to the pier at Douglas Harbour. The lamp on the right doesn't lean; its appearance is caused by the wide-angle of the lens. 11 October 2014

suspended operations. It re-opened for the 1919 season, with operation continuing until 1939. Services were again suspended during the Second World War but re-opening was not accomplished until the 1949 season, with the summer service continuing until the end of the 1953 season. As with the ferry service, the new bus service provided to Douglas Head from 1950 reduced the railway passenger numbers and profitability. The line and its equipment were sold for scrap during 1954, with removal taking place during October and November 1955.

Above: a poor but rare photograph of one of the Incline Railway cars at the upper station just below Douglas Head. (Courtesy of Travel Lens Photographic)
Right: the site of the upper terminus of the Incline Railway is now overgrown but its location is clear. 11 October 2014

Local bus services

Until 1976, when all bus services were taken over by the nationalized Isle of Man Transport, Douglas Corporation operated local bus services in and around Douglas. The Corporation's yellow livery with maroon bands was distinctive and contrasted with the maroon of the Isle of Man Road Services fleet that served the rest of the island. In 1949 Douglas Corporation introduced a new service between Lord Street Bus Station and the Battery Pier, near the lower end of the Incline Railway.

The following year the bus service was revised to operate to the top of Douglas Head, with the route running over the Stone Bridge at the west end of the harbour before making the ascent of Head Road – a fairly circuitous route a little over a mile long.

The competing bus service severely affected the economics of the harbour ferries and the cliff lift. Potential travellers could now board a bus near Douglas town centre or the railway station and be taken directly to Douglas Head with no need to walk to the pier, cross the harbour and wait for the cliff lift. The convenience and low cost quickly led to a cessation of the traditional leisure route to Douglas Head. The ferry and cliff lift owners were less than impressed with Douglas Corporation's competition.

DOUGLAS HEAD   **ROUTE 25**

OPERATES 19th MAY to 13th SEPTEMBER, 1974.

MONDAY TO SATURDAY

From Central Bus Station		From Douglas Head	
10.05 a.m.	4.05 p.m.	10.20 a.m.	4.20 p.m.
10.35 a.m.	4.35 p.m.	10.50 a.m.	4.50 p.m.
11.05 a.m.	5.05 p.m.	11.20 a.m.	5.20 p.m.
11.35 a.m.	6.35 p.m.	11.50 a.m.	6.50 p.m.
12.05 p.m.	7.35 p.m.	12.20 p.m.	7.50 p.m.
12.35 p.m.	8.35 p.m.	12.50 p.m.	8.50 p.m.
2.05 p.m.	9.35 p.m.	2.20 p.m.	9.50 p.m.
2.35 p.m.	10.35 p.m.	2.50 p.m.	10.50 p.m.
3.05 p.m.		3.20 p.m.	11.05 p.m.
3.35 p.m.		3.50 p.m.	

SUNDAYS

From Central Bus Station		From Douglas Head	
10.05 a.m.	5.05 p.m.	10.20 a.m.	5.20 p.m.
10.05 a.m.	6.05 p.m.	11.20 a.m.	6.20 p.m.
12.05 p.m.	7.05 p.m.	12.20 p.m.	7.20 p.m.
1.05 p.m.	8.05 p.m.	1.20 p.m.	8.20 p.m.
2.05 p.m.	9.05 p.m.	2.20 p.m.	9.20 p.m.
3.05 p.m.	10.05 p.m.	3.20 p.m.	10.20 p.m.
4.05 p.m.		4.20 p.m.	

ROUTE — Bus Station, Lord Street, Ridgeway Street, North Quay, Stone Bridge, South Quay, Gasworks Hill, Head Road, Douglas Head.

FARE STAGE — Quarry.

SERVICE FREQUENCIES WILL BE INCREASED ACCORDING TO DEMAND.

Above: An extract from the Douglas Corporation Bus Timetable for 1974-5 for service 25 between Douglas and Douglas Head. Note the provision of more buses according to demand. (Courtesy of Travel Lens Photographic) Left: Douglas Corporation AEC Regent No 62 (JMN 726) breasts the top of the first part of the climb up Head Road. The bus was delivered in 1948 and was fitted with a Northern Counties body. (Courtesy of Travel Lens Photographic)

Above: at the Douglas Head terminus the chock is under the front wheel of another AEC Regent with Northern Counties bodywork. No 59 (HMN 690) is one of a batch purchased in 1947. Behind the bus to the left is the road leading to the Marine Drive. (Courtesy of Travel Lens Photographic)
Left: no-waiting restrictions in the form of yellow lines now invade the road and buses are absent. 30 August 2014

The days of catching a number 25 bus to or from Douglas Head are also now long past. Buses still find their way along the South Quay *en route* from the present Banks Circus depot to Lord Street over the lifting bridge, but no longer serve Head Road. Meanwhile pedestrians face a stiff climb up the road, the steps opposite the lifting bridge or the pathway beside the old cliff lift. The direct route by foot crosses the lifting bridge over the harbour which reduces the distance to around three-quarters of a mile from the town centre.

At Douglas Head the turning circle used by terminating buses is still visible near the remains of the Incline Railway's upper station; beyond here the road continues towards the Marine Drive. This point also marked the start of the Marine Drive tramway, but as the last tram had left Douglas Head several years before the first bus arrived this was not the convenient interchange that it might have been.

In the late 1880s hopeful entrepreneurs proposed a Marine Drive along the rugged coast south of Douglas Head, along with a number of complementary ventures to increase the public's ease of access to them from Douglas town. Their hope was that the tolls collected would give the promoters a good return on the cost of building the Drive.

Douglas had grown up around the natural harbour and river which formed a barrier between the town and Douglas Head to the south. The Douglas Head Marine Drive Ltd. was formed on 1 July 1889 with the aim of building a carriage and pedestrian route between Douglas Head and Keristal, about three miles along the coast to the south. Access from Douglas to the Marine Drive was also desirable. In 1889 any thoughts of a tramway were clearly still in the future. As the route of the drive lay entirely within land owned by Major J.S. Goldie-Taubman of Nunnery House, Douglas, no land acquisition costs would arise and the landowner would receive income from any tolls collected. The company erected the impressive toll gate and gateway which still stands at the northern end of the Drive, although the gatekeeper's residence has now been demolished.

A postcard showing Douglas Bay from Douglas Head, with a car on the Incline Railway. The Great Union Camera Obscura is in the foreground and the tramcar is on the upper section of line

After much blasting of rock the contractors succeeded in constructing the new road high above the shore to just short of the cleft at Walberry, about one and a half miles to the south of Douglas Head. A substantial timber bridge was erected over Pigeon Stream.

Unfortunately these efforts exhausted the available capital. Douglas Head Marine Drive Ltd. passed into receivership and construction stalled during the autumn of 1891.

The company and its assets were acquired by a group of businessmen from Lancashire, England, on 12 March 1892, and an injection of extra capital allowed work to restart. Large wooden bridges were erected over the chasms of Walberry and Horse Leap, but were short lived as they were replaced by stronger steel girder bridges when the tramway was constructed only four years later. By autumn 1893, the drive extended to Little Ness, a total of about two miles from Douglas Head, the relatively flat area here affording a suitable space for a viewpoint and a carriage turning circle. The opening of the Marine Drive was celebrated in style with a banquet and speeches in a marquee at Little Ness on 7 August 1893. Work on the carriage drive beyond Little Ness continued during 1893 and the roadway was completed through to Keristal by November.

Right: waiting at the Douglas Head terminus is motor car 7. To the right is the booking office. The disk with the number 5 hooked onto the end dash indicates that the five-car service is in operation today (see page 29). (Courtesy of Travel Lens Photographic)
Below: the rocky outcrop shows that the approach to the Marine Drive is still easily identified. The building is residential accommodation 'The Point'. 30 August 2014

Construction of the tramway

In 1893 the Douglas Head Marine Drive company awarded a concession to build an electric tramway along the Drive. The concessionaires for this tramway had no connexion with the Isle of Man Tramways and Electric Power Company, who were dedicated to promoting what was to become the Manx Electric Railway between Douglas and Ramsey, and the Snaefell Mountain Railway.

The Electrical and General Contract Corporation of London, England, constructed the Marine Drive tramway under what modern parlance would describe as a design, build and operate contract, with a proposed initial period of ten years, which could be extended by a further twenty-one years unless the Douglas Head Marine Drive Ltd. decided to operate the line themselves. A thirty-year concession was finally agreed, commencing in 1896.

The driving force behind the Electrical and General Contract Corporation was William Sebastian Graff-Baker, an American engineer from Baltimore who had been the British agent for the Thompson-Houston Company of Boston, Massachusetts. He had been involved in other early British electric tramway ventures, including the commissioning of the pioneer Leeds line to Roundhay Park in 1891 and constructing the electric tramways of Coventry. The Graff-Baker family evidently had engineering in the blood as W. S. Graff-Baker junior, the son of the Marine Drive tramway

Seen from the deck of the MV Karina, *the 1891 Marine Drive gateway looms impressively. The location of the former gatekeeper's dwelling is clearly shown by the outline of the gable end (see page 14). 20 August 2014 (Sara Goodwins)*

engineer, later became the Chief Mechanical Engineer of London Transport Railways and President of the Institution of Locomotive Engineers.

At the end of the nineteenth century the Marine Drive still suffered from a lack of easy access from Douglas, so the Marine Drive company gained permission from the Goldie-Taubman family to construct a further tramway between Douglas Head and the South Quay. With the gradients involved there could be no reliance on adhesion so either a cliff lift or funicular would have been required. Although approved, this line was never constructed. An alternative plan to extend the tramway down to the harbour, across the Stone Bridge and back along the North Quay to the Victoria Pier also failed to materialize. This would have linked Douglas Head with the railway station and the Victoria Pier and the horse trams on the promenade.

The General Traction Company, another Graff-Baker organization, acquired the rights to the Marine Drive tramway on 20 March 1895. The Douglas Southern Electric Tramways Ltd (DSET), a wholly owned subsidiary of the General Traction Company, was set up on 21 October 1895 to become the operating company. Construction of the tramway started on 30 December 1895. The resident engineer, Mr. Lavington Fletcher, had previously supervised the construction of the Coventry Tramways, owned by the same group of companies. The General Traction Company also owned the Norwich Tramway Company and photographs show that the traction poles used on that system were similar to those of the Douglas Southern. These three systems comprised the General Traction Company's British operations and all three used a similar livery for their tramcars. The company evolved into the New General Traction Company on 24 March 1896 and also held assets in the United States of America.

Graff-Baker was conversant with American practice and as at this early stage of electric tramway development in the British Isles, local industry had not yet developed the capabilities to produce equipment for the novel form of transport, much of the overhead was supplied from established American manufacturers (see page 23).

Early electric tramways needed to generate their own power as the transmission of current over long distances was not then practical. In addition the Douglas Southern Electric Tramway predated commercial supplies on the Isle of Man. Concurrently with the construction of the tramway therefore, a coal-fired power station was built adjacent to Pigeon Stream, using the only easily accessible fresh water supply along the line. In dry weather sea water could be pumped up to augment the supply from the stream. The location was not ideal for fuel supplies, which were brought in by horse and cart, involving, as it did, the steep climb up Head Road from Douglas Harbour. The power station was equipped with two dynamos of 100kW for a total capacity of 200kW.

The original power plant suffered a blown cylinder cover in 1919, which reduced the available power output and had an adverse effect on the tram service. When there were sufficient passengers it had been normal to use trailer cars, but the

Below: the impressive two-span steel viaduct carrying the tramway at Walberry seen from the north. The masonry support to the central pier is not visible in this view. The shorter span of Horse Leap Bridge is just visible beyond the viaduct. (Courtesy of Travel Lens Photographic)
Left: the southern pier of the viaduct is visible in the modern view. The replacement road has been cut into the cliff. 30 August 2014

electricity shortage meant that none was used during the 1919 and 1920 summers. To remedy the power deficiency the tramway purchased a second-hand Bellis and Morcom Westinghouse steam generating set from the Farnworth Electric Light and Traction Company of Farnworth, Lancashire, England. This set had been superseded in its original location when Farnworth's supply was provided by the Lancashire Electric Power Company in 1918. Dating from 1903 the generating set arrived on the Marine Drive in July 1921 and was commissioned in September. This unit, rated at 250kW, then became the Douglas Southern's main power supply with the former plant being used as a standby. The increase in maximum power output over the original installation removed the restriction on trailer operation.

In 1935 the tramway started purchasing its power from Douglas Corporation, as the ability to transmit electricity over larger distances using high tension alternating current had become practical. Two new Hewittic rectifiers at Pigeon Stream were fed from the 3.3kV AC supply. As each rectifier had a capacity of 125kW the power requirements matched the nominal capacity of the displaced Bellis and Morcom unit installed in 1921. In effect the power station had now become an electricity sub-station and supplying coal to this inconvenient location was no longer necessary. The steam plant was broken up in 1936-7 and the boilers were sold to a buyer in Greece during 1938.

The steelwork for the bridges at Pigeon Stream,

Above: looking back from near Walberry the 60ft chimney of the Pigeon Stream power station looms incongruously over the cliffs. Beyond, the Marine Drive gateway can be seen. (Courtesy of Travel Lens Photographic) Right: a modern view looking back towards Douglas Head no longer shows the power station chimney. In the distance the twin towers of the ornamental gateway are still clearly visible, however. 30 August 2014

Walberry and Horse Leap was fabricated and erected by the Manchester, England, firm of Heenan, Froude and Company over a period of nine months. Heenan, Froude specialized in structural steelwork and were well-respected for building bridges and pit-head gear. Probably their most well known structure is Blackpool Tower which they erected in 1893. Evolution of the company has since seen the final divestment of its engineering interests to FKI and, as a shell company, Redman Heenan International was subject to a reverse takeover in 1986 by Clarke St Modwen. Rebranded as St Modwen it is now a major player in the property development business.

The Douglas Southern Electric Tramway's official opening ceremony was on 16 July 1896, despite having neither official inspection nor approval. Public service commenced on 7 August 1896, at first to the loop just to the north of The Whing and then through to Keristal on 5 September. At Keristal the Marine Drive turns back northwards to join the Old Castletown Road. The original plan had been to erect another impressive gateway, similar to that at Douglas Head, at the junction with the public road. Neither the gateway nor the plan to extend a branch of the tramway along this part of the Drive materialized, possibly due to a lack of finance. A much less imposing bungalow with a corrugated iron hut was erected instead and this served as the registered offices of the Douglas Head Marine Drive Ltd.

Over the winter of 1896-7 the tramway was extended from Keristal to a point above Port Soderick, additional capital being raised to fund the extension and buy extra cars. At this time Port Soderick was being developed as a tourist attraction and additional revenue

Keristal, shown here, was the original terminus of the Douglas Southern Electric Tramway. The depot at Little Ness had no fresh water supply, so the can being loaded may be drinking water. (B.Y. Williams/Courtesy of Travel Lens Photographic)

was expected from increased passenger numbers. The extension to the Drive required three-quarters of a mile of new track. Rather than adding another bridge the Marine Drive company chose to fill in the Keristal gorge. The new line had additional passing loops at Keristal and at the new terminus located 180ft above sea level above Port Soderick. Public service duly commenced at the start of the summer season on 1 April 1897.

Tramway history and war closures

The Douglas Southern Electric Tramway closed for the duration of the First World War, with services coming to an abrupt halt amid a mass exodus of visitors at the height of the summer season in 1914. The Marine Drive itself remained open to foot and non-tramway traffic during the war, with a small amount of toll income being received. The tramway re-opened for the 1919 season.

The loss of four years' income was a major blow to the tramway finances and it was necessary to issue a mortgage debenture on its property and suspend dividend payments. Prior to re-opening the overhead wires were renewed, the major bridges were strengthened and other maintenance work carried out.

The New General Traction Company agreed to sell the Douglas Southern Electric Tramway to the Douglas Head Marine Drive Company at the termination of the original franchise in 1926. The Marine Drive and the tramway became one organization. The only visible effect was that the power cars were re-lettered on the upper deck decency panels to show the new owner's name in place of the old, with operation continuing much as before.

The New General Traction Company re-organized itself following the sale of its subsidiary becoming the General Consolidated Investment Trust Ltd. This duly became a PLC, finally being voluntarily liquidated on 31 December 1997. Like many companies the name and objectives had changed considerably over the years.

Tramway services continued to operate along the Marine Drive each summer up to 1939. The decline in revenue due to the shrinking tourist trade and increasing maintenance costs meant that the company struggled to make a profit in the immediate pre-war years and dividend payments dried up. The declaration of war on 3 September 1939 did not interrupt services immediately and trams continued to run up to the end of the summer season on 15 September.

The tramway was not formally closed, but sadly it failed to re-open after the Second World War. A number of contributory factors led to this, including the use of the area by the military authorities (see page 30). The Hewittic rectifiers were removed from Pigeon Stream on 12 September 1942, with an outstanding debt to Douglas Corporation of £840. The tramway had had no income since shutdown and major rehabilitation works to track and overhead, as well as reinstatement of the power supply would all have been needed to enable a resumption of services after the war. The unstable nature of the cliffs in the vicinity of Walberry and Horse Leap meant that both of these major structures would have needed expensive structural strengthening, as would the bridge at Pigeon Stream, which was in a poor state of repair. Post-war austerity and a general shortage of supplies and finance were other negative factors, and Port Soderick had lost much of its pre-war attraction to visitors.

In view of the marginal nature of the operation during the 1930s, any reinstated services would have been unlikely to show a profit. The assets of the Douglas Head and Marine Drive Company were disposed of to the Isle of Man Highways and Transport Board in 1946, the majority of the tramway track and overhead being removed in 1946-7. The Marine Drive company was finally dissolved on 12 January 1948.

As mentioned in the previous chapter, the opening of the Marine Drive as a roadway for carriages and pedestrians was celebrated in style with a banquet and speeches in a marquee at Little Ness on 7 August 1893. Among the directors' speeches it was announced that a concession had been granted to build and operate an electric tramway along the drive. This was a bold statement of intent as electric tramways were still in their infancy at the time, although, as the initial section of the Manx Electric Railway from Derby Castle to Groudle Glen was to open exactly one month later, the technology was not entirely alien to the audience. If there could be a tramway along the coast to the north of Douglas, then why not one to the south?

Unusually for the Isle of Man, the track gauge for the new Douglas Southern Electric Tramways Ltd. was 4'-8 ½ " (1435mm), i.e., standard gauge, rather than the narrow gauge of 3'-0" (914mm) already selected by the Isle of Man Railway, the Manx Northern Railway and the Manx Electric Railway. The Douglas Southern was unique on the island in its use of standard gauge. The track was 65lb-per-yard flat bottom rail, in 30ft lengths, bolted to steel sleepers, at 42" centres, resting on concrete pads. The choice of steel sleepers and concrete supporting blocks was unusual; normal British practice would have been wooden sleepers on stone ballast. Steel sleepers are prone to corrosion, especially in a coastal environment subject to salt spray, so this may not have been the wisest choice. Whether they were better than wooden sleepers, which tend to rot, is an interesting question.

Above: just south of the arch this postcard shows motor car 7 and a trailer heading for Port Soderick. Evidently the weather is fine and there is a good load on board
Left: car parking has replaced the tram tracks, but the location is clear. This is where one of the tramway loops was located, still visible by the increased width of the formation
30 August 2014 (Sara Goodwins)

Above: the impressive tollgate is seen in tramway days with the gates closed. The pedestrian access turnstile is visible and the dog is keeping a wary eye on the photographer. One of the ornamental ironwork gates seems to have been replaced by a more utilitarian item. (Courtesy of Travel Lens Photographic)

Right: The seaward structure has been removed and an examination of the underside of the right-hand arch will reveal the fixing points for the trolley wires.
11 October 2014

The single track was laid on the inland side of the Marine Drive, which was widened to accommodate the line where necessary. The tramway passed through the ornamental gateway, using the landward arch, leaving the other arch for carriage traffic. A turnstile was used to collect tolls from pedestrians and the location of this is still clearly visible inside the arch. Passing loops were provided at roughly quarter-mile intervals along the tramway, the majority being long enough to hold one motor plus trailer set. The exceptions were the loops at the Port Soderick terminus and that just south of the northern gateway arch which were longer, allowing for trailers to be detached and parked during periods of light traffic, but available when required.

Alexander Penney and Co. of London supplied the pointwork, which incorporated integral check rails which accommodated wide and deep flanges: the wheel profile of the cars was more akin to railway than tramway practice. With the separation of the road and tramway there was no need for grooved street track on this line. Although generally undulating, the worst gradient on the tramway was as steep as 1 in 10.5, on the descent from The Whing towards Keristal. The sharpest curves, at The Whing and Rebog, were 45 ft radius, and were both greased to reduce flange wear and noise.

The tramway overhead was supported at 20ft above rail height by short bracket arms carried on steel traction poles located to the landward side of the line which were supplied by Morris, Tasker and Company of Philadelphia, Pennsylvania. Overhead fittings were supplied through R.W. Blackwell and Sons Ltd., but mostly manufactured by Albert and J.M. Anderson of Boston, Massachusetts. As the tramway engineer, W.S. Graff-Baker, was American, his familiarity with transatlantic practice probably influenced this choice of suppliers.

The rugged coastline required a number of substantial bridges to be built to avoid the costs involved with major rock removal (see page 35). The first structure south of Douglas was at Pigeon Stream, adjacent to the line's power station. The Pigeon Stream bridge was 117'-0" (35.7m) long. A three-span lattice steel girder structure was erected adjacent to the original timber viaduct, which was adequate for the roadway but not for carrying trams. The timber bridge was later removed.

Above: this postcard, issued by the tramway, shows a car negotiating the curves at The Whing on its way to Port Soderick. Note the sharpness of the curve in the foreground

Left: the southern part of the drive roadway was originally narrower than the north. This corner approaching The Whing was widened during the road works between 1956 and 1963. 30 August 2014

Above: the remains of the power station and three-span steel girder bridge over Pigeon Stream and are seen in this post-war view. (Courtesy of Travel Lens Photographic)
Left: the bridge has been replaced by the embankment which carries the road. The power station has been demolished. Did the masonry find its way into the embankment?
30 August 2014

Below: the viaduct at Walberry seen from the south. Note the bend in the middle. (Courtesy of Travel Lens Photographic)
Left: a classic postcard view of a Douglas Southern tram on the Walberry viaduct (see also title page)

At Walberry, a mile south of Pigeon Stream, an impressive two-span steel girder bridge 256'-0" (78m) long also replaced the original wooden structure provided when the Marine Drive was constructed a few years earlier. Walberry's two spans were angled at 10 degrees to each other and constructed on a north to south descending gradient of 1 in 17. The total steel weight was 102 tons and a masonry pier supported the central lattice column.

Three hundred yards south of Walberry, Horse Leap was bridged by a single span lattice girder 120'-0" (36.6m) long on an easier gradient of 1 in 59.5, also falling north to south.

The depot at Little Ness

The tram depot at Little Ness was one of the most remote depots ever built by a tramway. The rugged nature of the terrain traversed by the line restricted the choice of locations so the level area of the headland at Little Ness had obvious attractions, despite its operational inconvenience.

Lying to the seaward side of the Marine Drive and tram line, the timber-framed corrugated-iron depot had four tracks, initially served by a traverser connecting them to the approach track which crossed the drive from the Douglas end of the depot. As originally constructed, the depot was 93ft long and 40ft wide, but, with the delivery of four additional cars in 1897, the building was extended by 17ft to 110ft, which just enabled four cars to fit on each of the shed roads. The entire passenger fleet was accommodated under cover, an essential requirement given the need to protect the cars during the winter when services were suspended.

The traverser was replaced by three sets of points in 1909, which meant that the trailer cars could now be shunted into and out of the depot by their power cars at start and end of the day. The pointwork was obtained by the removal of a couple of the passing loops in the line and reusing the track.

Due to the remoteness of the depot, for some years it was the practice to leave the last car of the night at Douglas Head (with the controller handles removed) so that its crew could return home. The early morning crew then picked up the car for the first shift next day. In later years this practice was discontinued and staff were left to their own devices to make their way to and from the Little Ness depot. A long walk or cycle ride in possibly bad weather.

The remoteness of the depot did not preclude it being the site of a notorious crime; indeed it may even have been a contributory factor. On 23 July 1931 a courting couple, Irene Livesay from Rochdale and Duncan Fleming from Glasgow, were shot and seriously wounded at Little Ness by John Collister, one of the inspectors of the Marine Drive tramway. After being shot Fleming grappled with Collister to try and take the shotgun, but was also stabbed. Collister then tried to throw Miss Livesay over the cliff. She escaped, and upon reaching the toll gate, summoned assistance. Both survived and Collister was found guilty of attempted murder in October and sentenced to seven years penal servitude off island. No motive for the attack was ever given.

Above: trailer 16, one of the four cars delivered to augment the fleet when the line was extended to Port Soderick in 1897, is seen outside the depot. The underframes of the additional cars were much simpler than those of the original cars (see page 34).
(Courtesy of Travel Lens Photographic)
Right: judging from the skyline and fence, trailer 16 would have been parked about here in the previous view.
The return to nature is complete. 30 August 2014

Tramway services

The tramway operated a variable frequency service, depending on passenger demand, generally running between the hours of 10:00 am and 7:30 pm. With single-line operation and the lack of visibility along the line, the loops to be used as passing places were determined by how many cars were running. On the leading end of each car a metal indicator served as a visual reminder to oncoming motormen of how many cars were in use. Each loop displayed one or more numbers indicating which services used that loop to pass. Motormen then knew where to wait and where they could proceed safely.

There is only one recorded collision in the tramway's history, this occurring near the close of service on 4 July 1909. A conductor was driving (unofficially) and met another car head-on having passed through the loop at The Farm (to the north of Walberry), where he should have waited, *en route* for the depot at around 7 pm. The two cars were damaged and the conductor broke his ankle: both he and the driver were dismissed, but there were no other injuries. Car 3 was badly damaged in the accident. The identity of the other car is not known. In order to maintain the active fleet of motor cars car 3 exchanged its equipment, motors and identity with trailer 11.

Tram services normally required four, five or seven cars, giving service intervals of 12-13, 10½ or 7½ minutes respectively. Depending on whether trailers were used, considerable flexibility was built into the service, an essential requirement considering the susceptibility of demand to weather conditions. In later

Right: car 2 after arriving at the Port Soderick terminus of the tramway. The passengers seem to be in a hurry to disembark. On the opposite side of the Marine Drive the footpath leading to the Port Soderick cliff lift will soon be busy. (Courtesy of Travel Lens Photographic)
Below: compared with the animated scene where car 2 is arriving, the former tram terminus is a quiet spot now. A footpath still leads down to the promenade at Port Soderick, however. 30 August 2014

days a six-car service could also be deployed. The method of informing the staff of a change in the number of cars deployed during the day is not known. On operating days spare trailers were stored on the long loop just south of the Douglas Head gateway, so that they could be collected and pressed into service to meet the passenger demand at Douglas Head if necessary. Although this meant that the trailers were handy it also meant that the loop was not then available for passing purposes. Eight trailers and eight motor cars for a line almost exactly three miles long enabled a service frequency of 10 minutes to be maintained, with an advertised journey time of 30 minutes.

The tramcars

The initial fleet of cars supplied to the Douglas Southern Electric Tramway comprised a total of twelve double-deck cars; six motor cars and six trailers. Structurally the motor and trailer cars were identical. Each car had cross-bench lower-deck seating with access to each row of seats from a footboard on the seaward side of the car. As the cars ran on the land side of the roadway, and could not be turned, the staircases at each end both gave access from the sea side of the car. The Douglas Southern trams were the only double-deck electric cars to run on the island and their unusual arrangement of cross-bench seating on the lower deck and mirror image staircases made their design unique. The operation of double-deck trailers, while not unknown elsewhere, was also unusual so this was another distinguishing feature of the tramway.

On the motor cars the trolley mast was offset, being on the land side of the car rather than being placed on the centre line as would have been normal practice elsewhere. Twin overhead wires were provided throughout the length of the line, so there were no frogs in the overhead.

In the initial fleet the motor cars were numbered 1-6 and the trailers 7-12. The extension to Port Soderick in 1897 required more trams. Four additional trailer cars were purchased and the original trailers 7 and 8 were retro-fitted with motors, trolley poles and control gear. The four new trailers were numbered 13-16, there now being eight motor cars (1-8) and eight trailers (9-16).

The first twelve cars were built by Brush Electrical Engineering Ltd. of Loughborough, England. The motor cars had a tare (unladen) weight of around 6 tons 6 cwt (6.3 tonnes) and were mounted on four-wheel Lord Baltimore No. 2 trucks of 78 inch wheelbase, supplied by the Baltimore Car Wheel Company. They were equipped with Westinghouse (Pittsburgh) Type 12A 25hp axle-hung nose-suspended traction motors with a cradle suspension intended to reduce the unsprung weight and hence the hammer blow on the rail joints. Westinghouse Type 28A controllers were fitted to the motor cars. The trailer cars had similar trucks, but, in the absence of motors and control gear, were considerably lighter.

A Douglas Head Marine Drive tramway ticket. This is an adult one shilling Evening Excursion return from Douglas Head to Port Soderick, which was half the price of the normal fare. The operator's name shows that the ticket was issued after 1926. Note the inscription which shows that the holder has, in effect, paid the toll to access the Marine Drive as well as to ride on the tramway. (Courtesy of Travel Lens Photographic)

A postcard view of Port Soderick from the cliffs to the south. The octagonal building is a camera obscura and the Cliff Lift is operating. It is just possible to make out the route of the electric tramway as it traverses the cliffs in the background

The car livery was a combination of deep red and white or cream. The red was lined out in gold, with a reflected white line, although this was simplified in later years. Black underframes with grey steps and decks completed the presentation. Officially the cars were subject to a blanket 8 mph speed limit, but a single motor car with no trailer could easily exceed this and on the downhill sections of line faster running was not difficult.

The lower decks of the cars had seating for thirty six passengers, accommodating four on each bench. Swing-over seat backs were fitted, although there were fixed benches either side of the end bulkheads. The upper deck had a centre gangway with transverse seats for thirty nine passengers, instead of the expected forty, the space occupied by the trolley mast on the land side resulting in the loss of one seat.

The motor and trailer cars had the same arrangement, irrespective of whether a trolley mast was fitted or not, retaining the option for conversion of the trailers to motor cars. The exchange of identities between cars 3 and 11 following the

1909 collision shows that conversion was practical. The cars were fitted with striped canvas blinds on the lower deck which could be drawn to combat inclement weather, or to act as sunshields.

The equipment fitted to cars 7 and 8 when they were motorized in 1897 differed from the rest of the fleet in that General Electric GE800B 27hp axle-hung nose-suspended motors were used with GE Type K2 controllers instead of the Westinghouse equipment supplied with the original six motor cars.

The four new trailer cars delivered in 1897 were again constructed by Brush, but the running gear now featured a simple trunnion design (see photograph on page 28) as opposed to the Baltimore trucks fitted to all the earlier cars. It is not known why this departure was decided upon as the Baltimore trucks were still in production, but perhaps it was felt that the cheaper construction would be sufficient given that the trailers were unlikely to see such heavy use as the motor cars. The new trailers were lighter than the earlier ones and the more basic underframe tended to make the ride on them less comfortable.

All cars were fitted with chilled iron wheels, which are difficult to machine. In order to remove wheel flats developed during skids an alternative solution was provided. Affected cars were fitted with carborundum brake blocks supplied by the Wheel Truing Brake Shoe Co. of the USA. Remedial grinding took place in service with accompanying sound effects!

All Douglas Southern cars were mounted on single, four-wheel, trucks. As the Douglas Southern was operating a standard gauge line with many sharp curves this may seem surprising when the narrow gauge Manx Electric Railway opted for double bogie, eight-wheel, cars. As the Douglas Southern Electric Tramway was purely a tourist attraction, with a limited summer season over a short distance, high operating speeds were not essential, so the simplicity and economy of the single-truck design may have swayed the decision.

Initially there was a conductor on each car, so a crew of three was employed for a motor car and trailer set. Separate conductors for the trailers were not provided after the first few years of operation with consequent cost savings. Tickets were sold at the Douglas Head and Port Soderick booking offices, initially at rates of one shilling return or seven pence single. A break of journey was permitted at no extra cost. As the trams would need to slow or stop at the loops, it is presumed that passengers could join or leave the trams at any loop. By 1910 the single fare paid on the cars was higher, at 9d, than that paid at the ticket offices, encouraging passengers to pre-book: it seems likely that this increase may have been introduced at the same time as the reduction in conducting staff.

As the tramway passengers had access to the Marine Drive the fares collected incorporated the 1d toll which a pedestrian would have paid. In addition to the pedestrian tolls the tramway company also paid 5% of its gross receipts to the Marine Drive Company. At Douglas Head a car was always kept waiting to tempt passengers on board rather than have them start walking.

As stated in the previous chapter, operations ceased on 15 September 1939, shortly after the outbreak of the Second World War. The final day is reported to have used the minimum three-car service, with light traffic and a bitter wind blowing in from the sea. After the service finished the cars were stored in Little Ness depot. The next day the electricity supply was disconnected and the windows shuttered with the doors locked and barred. In the air of uncertainty of those days no one knew when, or if, the tramway would re-open.

During the Second World War the area south of Douglas was largely given over to the armed forces as a training area, and hence out-of-bounds to civilians. The Royal Navy took over Douglas Head and the coast to the south as part of *HMS Valkyrie*, a radio direction finding (radar) unit.

The Royal Air Force's No 1 Ground Defence Gunnery School was installed at Ronaldsway in July 1940, transferring to the Admiralty in May 1943 as *HMS Urley* (*urley* being Manx for Eagle). Ronaldsway then became the training base for RN squadrons 705, 710, 713 and 747. Many of the Royal Navy's Barracuda reconnaissance and torpedo planes were deployed on the bombing and torpedo range off the east coast of the island, with monitoring posts being placed along the Marine Drive. Locally, Port Soderick became known as Barracuda Bay, sadly on account of the number of crashes from planes of this type which failed to pull out in time.

An RAF Anson plane from RAF West Freugh, Wigtownshire, Scotland flew into the cliff in fog and snow about 40ft above the Horse Leap viaduct on 30 December 1943. The five crew members were killed and debris fell onto the viaduct.

With the end of the war the armed forces withdrew, and *HMS Urley* was decommissioned in 1946. Subsequently the Isle of Man Government purchased Ronaldsway which is now, of course, the island's commercial airport.

The tram fleet was stored in the depot after the end of the 1939 season and remained there for the duration of the Second World War. Although services did not resume, the fleet remained incarcerated until 1951, somehow escaping the attentions of the scrap metal merchants who had recovered the track and overhead from the Marine Drive. A group of transport enthusiasts purchased Douglas Southern Electric motor car 1 for preservation, this being one of the earliest occasions when private individuals bought a tramcar. The

Left: from the south the tram track can be seen climbing towards the two steel bridges at Horse Leap and Walberry.
(Courtesy of Travel Lens Photographic)
Above: comparison with the previous photograph shows that the cliff face has been cut back to make way for the roadway, which was built between 1956 and 1963. 30 August 2014

Left: motor car 1 outside the Little Ness depot, probably shortly before it was rescued by the preservationists in 1951. (Courtesy of Travel Lens Photographic)

Below: car 1 in its restored condition in the depot at the Crich Tramway Museum in Derbyshire. Its companions in this view include cars from Glasgow (left), Sheffield (behind) and Newcastle-upon-Tyne (right). (Courtesy of Travel Lens Photographic)

tram was extricated from the depot using the Douglas Corporation horse tram road trailer in June 1951. For the occasion the trailer was fitted with a short length of standard gauge track, and power was provided by a pair of Aveling-Barford heavy duty dump trucks loaned by the Highways Board. Negotiating the tortuous descent through Rebog and Keristal without rails was not easy.

Car 1 spent the next four years at the Highway Board's Quarter Bridge depot before it was shipped to London to join the exhibits in the British Transport Museum located

in the former London County Council Clapham tram depot. The British Transport Museum closed on 23 April 1973 and the collection was dispersed. Although car 1 still belongs to the national collection, it has been on long-term loan to the National Tramway Museum in Crich, Derbyshire where it arrived on 13 March 1975. Unfortunately the deep wheel flange profile used on the Marine Drive precludes its use in service at Crich, where the track comprises traditional grooved tram rail, as used on street tramways, which can only accommodate shallow profile flanges. Like many historic tramcars, car 1 has now spent more time in preservation than public service. Sadly, plans to preserve a matching trailer came to nothing. In the museum stock list, car 1 is stated to be the oldest overhead trolley equipped car at Crich, although older cars remain in regular daily service on the Manx Electric Railway.

During the winter of 1951-2 the remainder of the tram fleet was broken up on site. The Little Ness depot was demolished and the tower wagon and a flat truck which had been used for engineering purposes were also disposed of.

In 1960 the pointwork from the depot access was also recovered and taken to the Crich Tramway Museum in Derbyshire where it was re-laid. It now provides part of the access trackwork to the depot, so in one sense car 1 may feel at home. The greater tolerances on flange depth for the former Douglas Southern pointwork is no impediment to the Crich operating fleet with its shallower street tramway flange profile.

Many of the Douglas Southern traction poles were purchased by the Manx Electric Railway and can still be seen along that line. They are distinguished by cast collars where the cross-section changes. The poles are generally in good condition considering their exposure along either tramway for nearly one hundred and twenty years.

Building the motor road

Towards the end of the Second World War Tynwald had expressed an interest in acquiring the Douglas Head and Marine Drive Company's assets as part of a plan to preserve and promote the island's areas of natural beauty. The Marine Drive would then come under the control of the Highways and Transport Board, who wished to turn it into a public road capable of taking heavy traffic. The fifty year old bridges at Pigeon Stream, Walberry and Horse Leap were inadequate for heavy road traffic so the Board planned to remove them and cut back the cliffs to allow the construction of a widened road. The proposals were costly and the Highways and Transport Board did not finalize its scheme until September 1952. Presumably there were delays in gaining financial approval as work only commenced in 1956. The road was finally completed in 1963, 24 years after the tramway closed in 1939. The budget for the works was exceeded by a factor of three, which reflects the difficulties encountered. The road as completed is substantially what remains to this day.

Douglas Corporation introduced a bus service along the Marine Drive when the new road opened, possibly with an eye to improving custom at Port Soderick, where they had purchased the hotel in 1956, despite it lying well outside the borough boundaries. Buses ran north to south between Douglas Head and Port Soderick, the return journeys operating via the Old Castletown Road. As the road was relatively

One of the poles salvaged from the Marine Drive and reused on the Manx Electric Railway. This is pole 763 still in use at Ballajora. 4 August 2013

35

Douglas Corporation Transport Leyland Tiger Cub approaches Pigeon Stream bound for Port Soderick on service 15. The batch of eight Duple bodied Leyland Tiger Cubs was obtained second hand from Lancashire United Transport in 1970. (Courtesy of Travel Lens Photographic)

Extract from Douglas Corporation Transport's 1974-5 timetable for service 15 between Douglas and Port Soderick. The caveat about the weather and the possibility of increased frequency according to demand means that the actual service may be unpredictable. (Courtesy of Travel Lens Photographic)

PORT SODERICK   **ROUTE 15**

OPERATES 19th MAY to 8th JUNE, 1974, and
           9th SEPTEMBER to 13th SEPTEMBER, 1974.

DAILY

From VILLA MARINA (opposite War Memorial) and via MARINE DRIVE

10.00 a.m.	2.00 p.m.	7.00 p.m.
10.20 a.m.	2.20 p.m.	7.45 p.m.
10.45 a.m.	2.45 p.m.	8.30 p.m.

Extra Journey OUT via Castletown Road — 12.15 p.m.

From PORT SODERICK — IN via CASTLETOWN ROAD

10.25 a.m.	2.25 p.m.	7.25 p.m.
10.45 a.m.	2.45 p.m.	8.10 p.m.
11.10 a.m.	3.10 p.m.	8.55 p.m.
12.35 p.m.	4.20 p.m.	9.30 p.m.
	5.00 p.m.	10.15 p.m.
		11.00 p.m. NS

NS — Not Sundays.

OPERATES 9th JUNE to 8th SEPTEMBER, 1974.

DAILY

From VILLA MARINA (Opposite War Memorial)

X 9.40 a.m. A	12.15 p.m.	X 7.00 p.m. A
10.00 a.m.	X 2.00 p.m. A	7.20 p.m.
X 10.25 a.m. A	2.20 p.m.	X 7.45 p.m. A
10.40 a.m.	X 2.45 p.m. A	8.40 p.m.
	4.15 p.m.	

X — via Marine Drive.

From PORT SODERICK

10.05 a.m. A	2.25 p.m.	7.25 p.m. A
10.20 a.m.	2.40 p.m.	7.40 p.m.
10.50 a.m. A	3.10 p.m. A	8.10 p.m. A
	4.00 p.m.	9.00 p.m.
12.05 p.m.	4.20 p.m.	9.20 p.m. A
12.20 p.m.	4.40 p.m.	9.40 p.m. A
12.35 p.m.	5.00 p.m.	10.15 p.m.
		11.00 p.m. NS

All journeys except those marked "X" via Castletown Road in each direction.

A — Liable to be withdrawn in adverse weather conditions.

NS — Not Sundays.

SERVICE FREQUENCY WILL BE INCREASED IN EACH DIRECTION ACCORDING TO DEMAND.

narrow with sharp bends it was deemed inadvisable for buses to pass on the drive. Coach tour operators also followed the north to south convention, although the drive was open to traffic in either direction. The bus service started at the Villa Marina on Douglas Promenade and terminated at the turning circle just above the Port Soderick promenade and near the attractions. Some additional outbound journeys operated to Port Soderick via Old Castletown Road instead of the more scenic Marine Drive route. Outward journeys by either route carried the same service number – 15.

The final return journey to Douglas was at 23:00 (except Sundays). The agreement with the licensee of The Anchor at Port Soderick was that the driver would enter the premises so that a bell could be rung to alert drinkers not so much about closing time, but that their last bus ride back to Douglas would be departing shortly. Unfortunately, if a new driver were assigned to this service he might not know of the arrangement and the bell might not be rung. It was not unknown for the bus to return without all its intending passengers who were then left to find their own way home.

Due to the restricted headroom of the Marine Drive gateway on Douglas Head, the service on the Marine Drive was operated by single deck vehicles, although services via Old Castletown Road, and those turning at Douglas Head itself, were not restricted in this way. The final date of the Marine Drive bus service is not known, although official accounts put it as 1976. As the operation was seasonal then the last bus may have run at the end of the 1975 season, rather than during the 1976 season. The nationalized Isle of Man Transport took over the bus fleets and operations of the Isle of Man Road Services and Douglas Corporation Transport in October 1976, so Isle of Man Transport have never operated services along the Marine Drive.

The continued instability of the cliffs around Walberry, and the lack of demand for through traffic, meant that the road was closed as an official through route to all motorized traffic from 1976, it being felt that further major maintenance expenditure was unjustifiable.

Port Soderick's current service (Spring 2015) consists of morning and afternoon school buses, also available to ordinary passengers, on schooldays, with two additional buses every Tuesday and Friday. No extra services run during the holiday season. Operation is usually by one of the small Mercedes-Benz Sprinter City 35 single deck buses which arrived on the island in 2014. The route no longer descends to Port Soderick itself, but turns in past the car park at the top of the hill. Like the resort, the bus service is but a shadow of its former self.

Above: Douglas Corporation Transport Leyland Tiger Cub No 36 (230 UMN) is followed by a Duple-bodied twin-steer Bedford Val coach just before Pigeon Stream.
(Courtesy of Travel Lens Photographic)
Left: the road is less busy in this recent view near the same spot. The top of the gateway structure can just be made out on the skyline to the right of the motorcyclist. 30 August 2014

The Marine Drive today

Today the site of the power station is the Pigeon Stream car park, and all the buildings have been demolished. The adjacent steel bridge was replaced by an embankment across the bed of the stream during the reconstruction of the Marine Drive after the tramway had closed. The well-respected Manx historian A. W. Moore states that Pigeon Stream takes its name from the fact that pigeons used to nest in the area. The reason for this attraction is not given, but it is the case

Above: the fate of the Horse Leap Bridge seems to be sealed with the gas cylinders in place to power the cutting torches and the tram track already removed. (Vic Nutton/Courtesy of Travel Lens Photographic)

Left: the abutment of the Horse Leap Bridge is visible in this recent view from the Drive. The new road was cut into the cliff behind it. 30 August 2014

Above: the power station and the three-span steel girder bridge at Pigeon Stream are still largely intact, but the scene is one of decay. Demolition is imminent in this post-war view. (Courtesy of Travel Lens Photographic)
Right: a car park is now where the power station used to be and the embankment carries the road across the Pigeon Stream. 30 August 2014

Left: another of the Douglas Corporation Transport Leyland Tiger Cubs, No 34 (227 UMN), on the Marine Drive north of Walberry, working to Port Soderick on service 15. (Courtesy of Travel Lens Photographic)
Below left: the modern view shows the seclusion of the Marine Drive; even the overhead wire route in the previous picture has now disappeared. 30 August 2014

that, during the nineteenth century, the poor supplemented their diet with rabbits and pigeons. Possibly some enterprising individual fed and snared the birds here?

The Marine Drive still holds interest for walkers and natural historians. From the cliffs it is not unusual for seals or basking sharks to be seen in the sea below. To seaward, near Pigeon Stream lies Stack Indigo. As well as being nesting grounds for sea birds, stacks like this are also excellent habitats for lichen, over one hundred species of which grow around the Isle of Man's coast. Sea spleenwort is a fern which likes to be splashed by the sea and grows at the base of the cliffs in this area.

Shortly before Walberry viaduct a rock outcrop named the Nun's Chair is located to the seaward side of the drive. Legend has it that misbehaving nuns from St. Bridget's Nunnery were sent to pray in penance on this conical rock until the sea had ebbed twice. St. Bridget's is now known simply as The Nunnery and was once the home of the Goldie-Taubman family who supplied the land for the Marine Drive.

The road remains open to motor vehicles to near Walberry from the north and to Little Ness from the south, with the intermediate section available only as a footpath and cycleway. Considering the instability of the rock strata, the degradation since 1976, when there was a major rock fall, is relatively minor, although loose rock is visible below the road. The cliff below Walberry has also eroded and the current fence posts are set into the tarmac of the 1963 roadway. The absence of dwellings between the gateway on Douglas Head and Keristal means no one is directly inconvenienced by the closure and the route forms a pleasant walk. Potentially the path could be severed by further erosion or cliff falls.

The cliffs at Walberry are particularly steep and reach a height of around 300ft above sea level, with the tramway and the Marine Drive at 267ft. Inland of this point are Walberry Farm and Hill and the tiny cove beneath the cliffs is called

Above: seen from the cliff top, the Walberry Viaduct has already lost its northern span. The masonry pier supporting the central tower can be clearly seen. This view makes plain some of the drama of the original tramway. However not only the tram ride but also the view is not now possible as the cliff has been cut back for the new road.
(Vic Nutton/Courtesy of Travel Lens Photographic)
Right: seen from the sea the location of Walberry Viaduct shows the Marine Drive at 267ft above sea level with the cliffs towering above. The viaduct's central masonry support is still in place, but the rusting remains of the steel girders lie at the water's edge.
20 August 2014 (Sara Goodwins)

Port Walberry. Royal Fern is a plant more associated with curraghs but can also grow in sea cliffs and caves. It may be found around Douglas Head lighthouse and also in Port Walberry. Other coastal plants which grow along the Marine Drive include red fescue, sea campion, sea maywood, thyme and English Stonecrop.

Talking about English, many of the names along the Marine Drive are of course Manx, but Horse Leap is resolutely English. According to tradition a pack of hounds fell down the chasm while chasing a hare, but the huntsman survived due to the efforts of his horse which made a prodigious leap to safety. However, as hares are usually hunted by people on foot with only one or two dogs each, the tale seems more likely to be a fabrication for tourists!

The Walberry Viaduct seen from the cliff top, showing the loss of the northern span and the tram track. In its heyday it must have been an incredible ride. Generally the track was removed 1946-7 with the traction poles following later as seen in this view from about 1950. (Vic Nutton/Courtesy of Travel Lens Photographic)

Little Ness is the only part of the drive where the road and tramway are set back from the sea, and marks a change in the geological formation of the island: to the south much of the rock comprises glacial drift, but this is less common to the north. The difference in the appearance of the rock is very marked. Inland of Little Ness lies the farm of Ballaslig, which was owned by Thomas Creer in 1867 and may still have been owned by him and his family when the Drive was built. Examination of the site where the car shed once stood shows the line of the approach track and a level area indicates where the depot once stood above the cliffs.

Beyond Little Ness, one of the steepest drops to the sea along the Drive occurs at a bay called The Whing. The name is probably derived from the Manx *quing* meaning a yoke or swingletree, which is attached to the traces of a draught animal and used to pull a vehicle. On the map the bay and the tram track have the shape of a swingletree at this point, rather like those the Douglas horse trams still use today.

Rebog lies shortly after The Whing. The name probably comes from the Norse *rabbi*, meaning a sand or gravel bank, which often forms a small bay. Gravel is a feature of the geology of the Marine Drive and is one of the reasons for its instabilities. Clay is also present at Rebog as a large deposit of glacial drift.

At Keristal the coastal section of the Marine Drive joins the inland part which runs to join Old Castletown Road. Heading south the drive takes a sharp left-handed bend and continues above the cliffs towards Port Soderick. At first sight Keristal appears to be a Norse farm name, possibly meaning rock valley or farm, given to a hamlet north-east of Port Soderick. The Manx version is Ballacreggan which is a farm north of Keristal. It is more probable that Keristal comes from *stallr* meaning a shelf, pedestal or cliff in Norse while a *kerling*, also Norse, is a rock protruding from the sea just off the shore. Whatever the derivation Keristal, indicates a very rocky place.

Keristal was the site of a wreck when the Dutch vessel *Grietje* was blown onto the rocks in a blizzard in 1963. Coastguard and rocket crew helped the eight members of the ship's crew climb the cliffs to safety, but the ship broke up. Parts of the wreck may still be seen on the shore, but only from the sea as the cliff overhangs. The only part of the Drive visible from the Isle of Man Railway is the section beyond Keristal and, of course, views of the railway are also possible.

Inland of the final section of the Drive between Keristal and Port Soderick, lie the farms of Ballamona and Ballashamrock, both parts of the Gresby treen. Ballamona was owned by Paul Leece in 1876 and may still have been owned by him and his family when the Drive opened. Ballashamrock was owned by the Quayle family of Castletown, who also owned Crogga house, just up the hill from Port Soderick. They never lived at Crogga but used it as a base to store smuggled goods. Port Soderick was ideal for smuggling, having a good harbour near a large town, but with few inconvenient buildings overlooking it.

Street sign at the junction between Marine Drive and Old Castletown Road. The road numbering of the Marine Drive has changed over the years. On some maps Marine Drive begins at Douglas as the B80, becomes unclassified where it is unsuitable for motor vehicles and then becomes the B52 between Keristal and Old Castletown Road. On other maps the B52 has been subsumed into the A37. The street sign seems to agree with the latter opinion. 19 February 2015

Port Soderick Cliff Lift

The cliff lift at Port Soderick had originally been installed as the Falcon Cliff Lift in Douglas, operating there from 6 August 1887, but becoming disused by 1896. It was re-erected at Port Soderick during 1897. The gauge was 4'-0" and, as the line needed to be longer than the previous installation, additional material was used in its construction. New cars also were provided, although the original Falcon Cliff car bodies were re-used as kiosks on the Port Soderick promenade. Like the Douglas Head Incline Railway (see page 9) the lift was driven by an oil-powered engine at the top of the incline, with the cars counterbalanced on a cable. The fare was 1d down and 2d up.

Below: Port Soderick, showing the cliff lift climbing behind and beyond the promenade. The tramway terminus was at the top of the hill beyond the upper station. Note that the Forrester family, the resort owners, do not use the final 'k' in the spelling of Soderick. (Courtesy of Travel Lens Photographic)

Left: the modern view of the promenade at Port Soderick shows that little of the entertainments and facilities still exist. The line of the cliff lift is discernable, but even the 'new' Anchor public house is now boarded up and out of use. 6 September 2014

Left: the site of the lower station of the cliff lift. The steps are on the far side of the trackbed and form part of the footpath up to the Marine Drive.
6 September 2014
Below: looking up the steps shown in the previous photograph the trackbed of the cliff lift is still evident on the right nearly seventy years after the rails were removed. 6 September 2014

The derelict remains of the Falcon Lift in Douglas are those of the second cliff lift, installed by William Wadsworth and Sons of Bolton in 1927, and are on a different site from the lift taken to Port Soderick.

The Port Soderick Cliff Lift opened on 11 July 1898, a little over a year after the Douglas Southern Electric Tramway was extended to its new terminus above the budding resort (see page 20). The Cliff Lift then ran during the summer seasons, presumably matching the tramway's operating dates. Services were suspended during the First World War, probably closing at the same time as the tramway. The Cliff Lift re-opened for the 1919 season, and continued to operate each summer. Finally, it closed once again for the duration of the Second World War. Although again the date is not known, it seems likely that this was the same as for the Marine Drive Tramway, i.e. 15 September 1939. As with the tramway, the return to peace did not see the Cliff Lift re-opening and it was eventually dismantled for scrap during 1947-9.

Nowadays the route of the Cliff Lift is still clearly visible, and a footpath runs parallel to its course from the promenade towards the top of the hill, crossing under the route of the lift about half way up, and emerging onto the road near the site of the former Marine Drive Tramway terminus. The Cliff Lift route is largely overgrown: the stone pillars which supported the track remain but the timber has rotted away.

Port Soderick

In its heyday Port Soderick was very popular, and accessible from Douglas by competing modes of transport. The name of Port Soderick has nothing to do with cursing, although it may sound like it. It was originally thought to have come from *suðer-vik*, meaning southern creek, but experts now think the name derives from *saltbuðarvik*, which means salt-shed-creek. It was here that Norse settlers extracted salt from the sea by boiling off water.

The Isle of Man Railway's Port Soderick station is on the Douglas to Port Erin line and situated a short walk away up the glen. The coast route via Douglas Head and the Marine Drive Tramway, and coastal steamers provided alternative routes to the road access via the Old Castletown Road.

Above: double-deck buses could be used for services via the Old Castletown Road. Here we see AEC Regent V No 15 (410 LMN) using the turning circle by the south end of the Port Soderick promenade. This vehicle was the last double deck AEC bus to be built and was one of a pair with Willowbrook bodywork bought in 1968. Considering London Transport's policy of bulk buying from AEC it may seem odd that the final bus arrived on the Isle of Man. Happily this historic vehicle is preserved on the island (Courtesy of Travel Lens Photographic)
Right: the location of the turning circle is still readily identified, although service buses no longer use it. 19 February 2015

Above: this postcard view from the beach shows that the cliff lift operators were on the ball when it came to selling advertising space. The tramcars terminated at the top of the hill beyond the cliff lift's upper station

Left: the arch and the sea wall are clearly the same but much else at Port Soderick has changed. The route of the cliff lift is easily distinguished. The blue footpath sign points the way to the Raad ny Foillan, *the island's coastal path, which follows the Marine Drive to Douglas. 6 September 2014*

Right: Douglas Corporation Leyland Tiger Cub No 36 (230 UMN) at the turning circle at Port Soderick in 1971. The bus made its way to Port Soderick along the Marine Drive (see page 37) and is about to return to Douglas by the Old Castletown Road (Courtesy of Travel Lens Photographic) Below: the present-day route 29 buses turn by looping past the large car park at the top of the hill and do not use the turning circle by the promenade. The space occupied by the bus is now used for car parking. 30 August 2014

Port Soderick lies on the estuary of the Crogga River at the lower end of Port Soderick Glen. Local folklore places an island in the sea off Port Soderick which was drowned by the mythical Irish warrior Finn McCool after the locals unwisely insulted him. The island is said to resurface for half an hour every seven years. If anyone should manage to place a bible on it whilst it is above the sea then the island will be restored. It might ruin the offshore oyster bed though.

The remains of the oyster bed can still be seen below the south cliffs. One of the attractions of Port Soderick was a raised path above the bed where visitors could view the oysters *in situ*. They were a huge attraction to the cove but were something of a cheat – oysters do not grow naturally in Manx waters and the beds were restocked every spring!

Port Soderick also had the almost obligatory 'smugglers' cave'. Visitors could buy candles from one of the stalls on the beach front to explore it. The Forrester family who developed Port Soderick had previously been tenants of Laxey Glen Gardens and also owned the Victoria Café on Victoria Pier in Douglas. In its prime Port Soderick had a camera obscura, a pub, cafés and numerous stalls including an unusual attraction in the form of the padded cell reputed to be from the hospital of the ship *Olympic*, a sister ship of the *Titanic*.

As well as being accessible by the Marine Drive, the Forresters provided access to Port Soderick from Douglas by sea. A fleet of motor boats was gainfully employed in bringing the customers and their cash to and from the resort. Sea visits to Port Soderick distorted official government statistics, as passengers who returned from Port Soderick was classed a sea arrival at Douglas!

After the Second World War the resort gradually declined although an attempt was made to breathe new life into it when Douglas Corporation purchased it in 1956. The Corporation invested significant sums of money into the resort's revitalization, including providing bus services to and from Douglas from 1963. Douglas Corporation sold Port Soderick in 1985. Since then there have been various attempts to run the Anchor pub but at the time of writing (2015) no attractions remain open. The glen provides pleasant woodland walks by the Crogga River, but there is no sustenance or amusement to be had on the once bustling promenade.

A 1960s postcard shows that Port Soderick was at that time still a thriving resort. On the left is the turning circle shown on page 48

The Isle of Man Railway provides a summer service calling at Port Soderick station at the top the glen. Sadly the days of extra trains bringing crowds of visitors to the resort from Douglas are long past.

The *MV Karina*, although not the original vessel of that name, sails from Douglas in the summer season, and on some of her afternoon cruises along the east coast of the island, visits Port Soderick in the capable hands of Captain Stephen Carter. *Karina* proudly carries on the tradition of Manx pleasure boats.

Although Port Soderick and the Marine Drive may appear moribund they may perhaps be woken from their slumbers and regain some of their former glory. The coastal scenery is still stunning and the bay is pleasantly sheltered. Other Manx attractions have made unlikely comebacks so possibly this pleasant cove close to Douglas may yet re-awake.

The afternoon school bus has just arrived at the stop by the car park above Port Soderick. Mercedes-Benz Sprinter City 35, No. 142 (MAN 42H) was purchased in 2014. The driver is about to change the destination indicator for the return journey to Douglas. 19 February 2015

MAP

The sketch map below is intended only to give a general idea of the location of some of the places mentioned in the text. Those walking or cycling the route of the tramway would be advised to use the 1:50,000 Ordnance Survey (OS) Landranger Map, sheet 95 (the pink one). Walkers should use either the OS map or the 1:25,000 Public Rights of Way and Outdoor Leisure Map published by the Isle of Man Government.

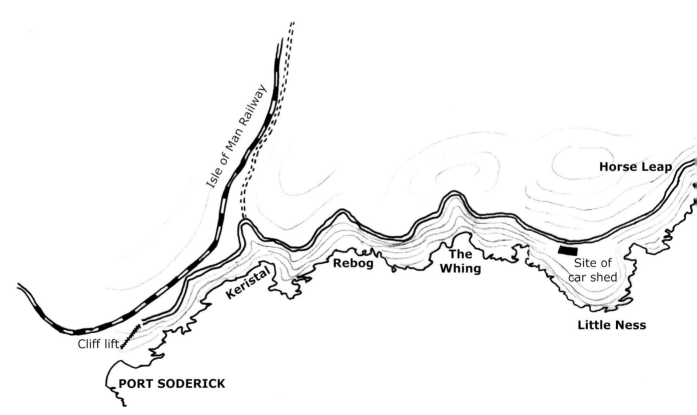

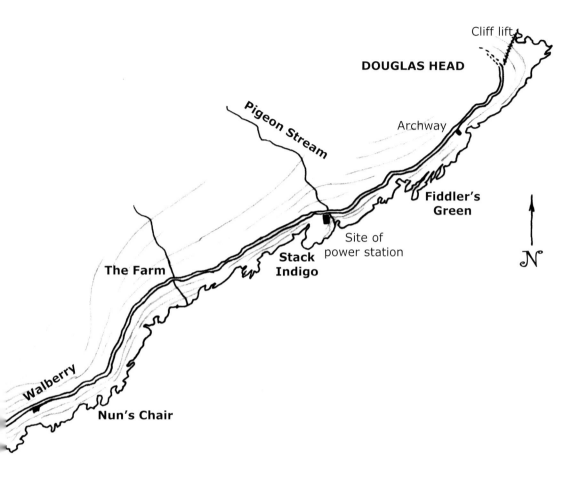

Today the Marine Drive forms part of the *Raad ny Foillan* (the Way of the Seagull), the long-distance footpath which hugs the coast of the Isle of Man. Ninety-six miles long, the *Raad ny Foillan* was first mooted in the early 1960s. Work started in the early '70s and the footpath was finally opened in 1986, when the island made special efforts to celebrate its heritage.

ACKNOWLEDGEMENTS

The author wishes to express his thanks to Tony Wilson of Travel Lens Photographic for his help and assistance in providing many of the historic photographs in this book. Thanks are also due to my wife, Sara Goodwins, for typesetting, constructive suggestions and encouragement.

SELECTED BIBLIOGRAPHY

Basnett, Stan & Pearson, Keith, *Double Century*, Adam Gordon, 1996

Carter, Stephen P., *Douglas Head Ferry and The Port Soderick Boats*, Twelveheads Press, 2003

Davis, Richard, *Buses of the Isle of Man 1945 – Present Day*, Lily Publications, 2009

Goodwyn, Mike, *Douglas Head Marine Drive and Electric Tramway*, Manx Electric Railway Society, 1993

Gray, Edward, *Manx Railways and Tramways*, Sutton Publishing, 1998

Hyde, W.G.S. & Pearson, F.K., *Isle of Man Tramways Album*, Douglas Cable Car Group, c. 1970

Pearson, F.K., *Isle of Man Tramways*, David and Charles, 1970

Pearson, F.K., 'The Douglas Head Marine Drive', *The Journal of The Manx Museum*, Volume VII, Number 86, 1970

Pearson, F.K., 'Douglas Southern Electric Railway, 1896', *The Journal of The Manx Museum*, Volume VII, Number 88, 1976

From the south end of Port Soderick beach at low tide, looking back at the cliffs along which the Marine Drive still runs